handing on the faith

Other **Handing on the Faith** titles:

Your Child's First Penance

Your Child's First Communion

Your Child's Confirmation

Baptism

_____

Child's Name

_____

Parents

_____

Godparents

_____

Date of Baptism

_____

Priest

_____

Church

_____

Address

_____

City, State

Your Child's Baptism

Carol Luebering

ST. ANTHONY MESSENGER PRESS
Cincinnati, Ohio

Nihil Obstat
Rev. Lawrence Landini, O.F.M.
Rev. Edward J. Gratsch

Imprimi Potest
Rev. Fred Link, O.F.M.
Minister Provincial

Imprimatur
+Most Rev. Carl K. Moeddel
Vicar General and Auxiliary Bishop
Archdiocese of Cincinnati
February 22, 2000

Cover and interior illustrations by Julie Lonneman
Cover and book design by Mary Alfieri

ISBN 0-86716-343-7

Published by St. Anthony Messenger Press
www.AmericanCatholic.org
Printed in the U.S.A.

Contents

Introduction

There is no miracle as moving as welcoming a child. Every infant is a wonder, but this wonder surpasses all others. All the months of anticipation and preparation, all the dreams that filled that time fall short of the wriggling warmth you hold at last. Even if this is not your first child, this baby is different from every other.

You have made an enormous commitment to the future. Your other relationships, your time, energy and space must all make room now for a demanding presence who will drain your financial and emotional reserves. This small person challenges all your certainties—first, your faith.

Perhaps your family and friends—even you yourself—take it for granted that this baby will be baptized. But full participation in the Rite of Baptism presumes more thoughtful preparation.

Parents are greeted with two questions as they present their child for Baptism: "What name do you give your child?" "What do you ask of God's Church for (name)?"

The answers are easy to speak. The struggle to decide the first is ended. The rite suggests an assortment of brief responses to the second: Baptism, faith, eternal life. But anyone who has ever spoken of love to another knows what a single word can hold.

The baptism of a baby encompasses many things:

1. initiation into the believing community,
2. the bestowal of a name,
3. the renunciation of evil,
4. the beginning of life in Jesus Christ.

Its meaning embraces concepts we understand only by degrees: faith, life, relationship, Church.

Finding truly expressive answers to the questions of the rite is only a beginning—the beginning of an ongoing exploration of the faith you hope to hand on to your child. The many levels of meaning that lie behind these answers are deeply rooted in your personal experience of God and Church and can be discerned only in prayerful reflection.

Your Child's Baptism offers help. It includes background thoughts on parenting and quotations from Scripture, the liturgy of the sacrament and the *Catechism of the Catholic Church* to ponder, as well as questions to guide your reflection and discussion.

A Process of Initiation

Following Jesus' command, the apostles baptized individuals and whole households. Tiny tots were probably included. While adults soon underwent a lengthy process (the catechumenate), infant Baptism today is the beginning of an even longer process of initiation that is completed with Confirmation and First Eucharist.

Called
by Name

A child is born a stranger. Thrust from comfortable warmth and darkness, your baby travels a long and perilous route to your welcoming arms. A confusing world lies at the journey's end. Eyes and ears and skin are assailed by new sensations; cold air fills lungs and is expelled with a cry.

Then your arms and voices speak tender welcome and the stranger is home. But birth is only the first journey, the beginning of a lifelong search for people who will recognize and welcome. "No one knows my name" is an expression of unbearable loneliness. No one, young or old, can be left in that emptiness and survive. In the nursery the lonely die; in nursing homes they decay. People need to be known, to be welcomed, to be called by name.

A name has no real meaning apart from a person. It is only a word until it is attached to a real person. Then it becomes inseparably a part of a person's identity, the first answer to the question, "Who are you?"

A name cannot easily be put aside or changed. An

immigrant may assume a name that flows more easily in a new tongue; a woman may take her bridegroom's name as her own. That action proclaims a profound change of identity and announces the beginning of a new life. Even the adolescent's rejection of an earlier nickname announces a new person.

So significant a gift cannot be lightly given. You discussed your baby's name for many months. And that struggle expressed your hopes and dreams for your child. You probably rejected many names in your search for just the right name, one which means for you strength or beauty, wisdom, tenderness or certain success in life. Your choice tells what you want your child to be.

Naming Your Child

Catholics traditionally pick a saint's name for Baptism. You choose this "patron saint" as a model you hope your youngster will imitate and as a heavenly advocate for the child. Canonized saints are the Church's greats, but the heavenly population includes many smaller lights— less famous folks who have touched your own life with their goodness.

Ultimately, of course, no one decides what another person will be. Each individual makes personal choices. But in the beginning, someone else must claim responsibility and authority and care for a budding life. You are that someone for this child, so you have the right to choose a name. Friends and family may suggest, but only *you* can choose.

Giving identity and claiming responsibility are profoundly human deeds. But most of all, the gift of a name signifies the holiest human experience: entering into a relationship.

When you speak your baby's name, you approach this small person intimately. Within a few months of birth, your baby's head will turn to the sound of the name you have chosen, the first word to acquire meaning. With a lopsided grin, your child will share the secret: Each of you knows your baby is someone very special.

A few months later your child will speak your name. In any tongue, the equivalents of *mommy* and *daddy* are usually the first words a child masters. *Mommy* and *Daddy*, not Peg and Mark or Maria and Tony. This tiny person will lay aside your old name for a new one—a single word that will always evoke your smile, your voice, your touch. All through life, your child will call you by the name that says what a special part you play in his or her life.

And you are changed. You carry a new identity, whether this is your first child or one of many. You will be Alice's father, Paul's mother for the rest of your life, bound in a relationship sometimes rewarding, sometimes frustrating, but always different from your relationship with anyone else.

From the beginning of history humans have sensed a greater being, someone who called the world into existence. The Jews called him Yahweh, "I Am Who Am." He is known as God and as Lord.

In time, a child was born and given the name Jesus, "God saves." When that child spoke God's name for us, he spoke in terms of relationship. "Father," he called him, "*Abba*"—a Jewish child's "daddy."

Baptism, too, is a birth, a long journey through darkness toward the light where the strong and gentle arms of Jesus' Father wait in welcome.

For Reflection and Discussion

- *What name have you chosen for this child?*

- *What names have you considered and rejected?*

- *What kind of person do you most hope your child will be? How does the name you have chosen reveal something of that wish?*

- *What difference does this baby make in your sense of who you are?*

- *When you pray, by what name do you call God? What relationship is reflected in that name?*

What name do you give your child? What do you ask of God's Church for (name)? (*The Rite of Baptism*, 76)

Can a woman forget her nursing child,
or show no compassion for the child
    of her womb?
Even these may forget,
yet I will not forget you.
See, I have enscribed you on the palms
    of my hands....
(Isaiah 49:15-16)

God calls each one by name. Everyone's name is sacred. The name is the icon of the person. (*Catechism of the Catholic Church*, #2158)

Circle of Community

Your baby claims the family name, the first assurance that this new life is already in relationship to others. Your family is your child's first community—the first people to speak the little stranger's name with love. The family is a child's primary source of love and support. Its members will applaud the first steps and kiss away bruises. As your child grows, your family will remain the first place to turn for assurance and celebration.

But the family cannot remain the only source of support. As a child grows, so does the need to take a place in widening circles of community. Your baby's first playmates will be the children of friends and neighbors; in a few years your child will be choosing special friends among classmates.

As an adult, you are a part of many communities. Beyond family and friends, you daily associate with neighbors and coworkers. Clubs, professional organizations and service groups also support relationships with others.

Baptism is also an entry into a community, a welcome into God's family. All people, of course, are God's family, the children God formed in love. God can no more refuse the parent/child relationship than you can deny your own parenthood. But not everyone knows God as a loving parent.

The people of the Church are God's family in a special way. They know who they are. They continue to explore the divine identity and to commit themselves to live as God's children, however imperfectly. They know God's dream of unity in the human family, their call to care for brothers and sisters in need.

Like all families, the Church is subject to stress and clumsiness in day-to-day living. As an institution, the Church can sometimes seem unlovable—restrictive, bureaucratic, unfeeling. That fact has turned many away from organized religion, even from belief in God—a failure regretfully acknowledged in the Vatican II document, *The Church in the Modern World.* Yet for millions of people it has the feel of home. All over the world, Catholics struggle to build community, to forge bonds of love and concern between people.

This is the family that makes your child its own in Baptism. It, too, bestows its name: Catholic.

An infant must grow into many names. A given name may be shortened to something more a baby's size. A baby gains a national identity before mastering the native language; years will pass before your baby can exercise all the rights of citizenship.

Every child learns early that certain expectations go with the family name. Whether or not the family down the street really lets kids eat candy any time, your child will learn your family's rules.

Catholic is also an identity to grow into. Neither the privileges nor the responsibilities associated with faith are fully a baby's own on the baptismal day. Baptism is only the first stage of your child's initiation into the believing community.

When adults or school-age children are baptized, the three sacraments of initiation—Baptism, Confirmation and Eucharist—are usually celebrated as one event. The new member of the community steps immediately into full participation in the life of God's family. But the infant whose personal faith is still only a promise on another's lips begins a longer initiation process that becomes increasingly a conscious involvement as the years go by. The three sacraments of initiation will be celebrated, like your baby's growth, in stages.

Human growth never occurs in isolation. From language basics to nuclear physics, people learn from others. You teach this baby to sort *mommy* and *daddy* out from the babble of sound. Your baby learns the sound of your own name from you.

To learn the name of God, your baby must first hear it from the lips of others—just as you did. Even more importantly, your child needs to *know* God, to feel divine love in the warmth of your arms, to see God's dream of unity and mutual care lived in the circle of family and Church. Where else can a child learn of God's love? Where can God's law be taught except where it orders the life of a family or a community?

The arrival of a baby sends ripples throughout a family. Snapshots fill mailboxes and computer screens. Everyone wants to know just who this newcomer is, what fresh version of family features has been created.

In the faith community, too, we note a family resemblance. Every Christian shares in the heritage of the whole Church. Yet the relationship between God and each unique child is marked and shaped by that uniqueness. From Thomas Aquinas to the present pope, from early martyrs to the cook who carries a casserole to a sick neighbor, each individual reflects a personal discovery about God and reveals a new dimension of divine love.

When your little one begins to explore the wonderful world God made, her wonder refreshes your own heart. Children's words clothe profound truths in fresh and simple language. Even the struggle to answer the questions your child will ask can lead you to deeper understanding of your own beliefs and enlarge your concept of God.

The first gift a child brings to the Church at Baptism is the helplessness of infancy. An infant at the font is a living reminder that life—even eternal life—is wholly a gift. In front of our eyes, this new life is given to one who has not as yet even thought about trying to "earn" it.

Believers are therefore asked to repeat their own baptismal vows—to reaffirm their dependence on God and their acceptance of responsibility for one another. They are asked to be a community of love for this child, your baby—and for you.

For if an individual does not grow in isolation, neither does a family. The influence of the surrounding culture seeps in. From Santa Claus to the drug culture, from patriotism to violence, the air is thick with other people's decisions about values.

The Christian community gathers at a baptism in support of the family. We will, their presence speaks, be part of the world your child discovers. We will show her

God's care for all human children. We will teach him thoughtfulness, kindness, goodness. We will know your child by name and speak that name with love.

Your child cannot be baptized without that pledge of support. You will not bear the sole responsibility for your baby's growth in faith. Beside you at the baptismal font will be other believers who pledge their help: the godparents you invite to walk with you.

Choosing Godparents

Godparent is not an honorary title but a job description. Godparents are, with you, a child's guide on the Christian life journey. They will help shape your little one's faith by sharing their own in word and deed. You will therefore want to choose people whose own baptismal commitment is firm and whose love for God and neighbor is generous.

The rest of the community needs to walk with you also. It may well be that the family that welcomes your child by name at Baptism does not know your own very well. The parish family is frequently clumsy in extending a welcome to new members. Young adults especially can feel isolated and unimportant in a parish whose attention is centered on educating children.

New opportunities for involvement will certainly open to you as your child grows. But even now the community has real need of your gifts, your talents, your witness to God's care for us. After all, you are one of those who know God's name. You can speak it with your brothers and sisters when the family meal is celebrated. The family of God knows clumsiness and stress as well as any other. But where else can we turn for assurance and celebration?

For Reflection and Discussion

- *Of what communities do you feel yourself really a part (family, Church, friends, coworkers...)? Where do they overlap?*

- *What special gifts do you bring to the communities to which you belong? (Don't say none without asking someone who loves you!)*

- *What ties do you have to your parish community?*

- *How does your parish meet your need to become involved (Sunday worship, study or prayer groups, opportunities for recreation, education service...)?*

- *When and where will your baby be baptized? Who will be present?*

(Name), the Christian community welcomes you with great joy. In its name I claim you for Christ our Savior by the sign of his cross. I now trace the cross on your forehead, and invite your parents (and godparents) to do the same. (*Rite of Baptism*, 79)

You are my witnesses, says the Lord,
   and my servant whom I have chosen,
so that you may know and believe me
   and understand that I am he.
Before me no god was formed,
   nor shall there be any after me.
(Isaiah 43:10)

In our own time, in a world often alien and even hostile to faith, believing families are of primary importance as centers of living, radiant faith. For this reason the Second Vatican Council, using an ancient expression, calls the family the *Ecclesia domestica* [the domestic Church].... "No one is without a family in this world: the Church is a home and family for everyone...." (*Catechism of the Catholic Church*, #1656, 1658)

A Decision Against Evil

You have a new place in the pages of history; you are a link between generations. Through the years ahead you may find yourself searching the family tree for a better understanding of your child's personality and talents—even faults.

You may blame relatives far and near for this child's quick temper or stubborn streak, or give them credit for a musical talent or a gentle disposition. You may delight in a shared gift or see your own faults reflected in your offspring.

You hope to see your baby grow into a wise and loving person, making the best possible use of all the ancestral gifts. God's dream for human children is not very different. The Creator made human beings in the divine image: capable of loving and giving life. Like any other parent, God would see us live in peace and harmony.

But somewhere before the beginning of recorded history, human hearts refused to warm with the Creator's love. Our earliest ancestors insisted on doing it their way. They made their own unwise decisions about good and evil. The first refusal was passed down through endless generations, and the human family's warmth was chilled by greed and anger, hatred and deceit.

This beautiful blue planet bears the scars. It is fouled by selfish exploitation, clouded with the smoke of countless wars. The division of God's human family into races, classes and nations, the uneven distribution at the table of earth's bounty threaten the lives of helpless children around the world. Something evil, something tangibly real and larger than life is loose on the earth.

All people are born under the shadow of that evil, alienated from one another and from God. At the dawn of consciousness, the ancient lie echoes in every human heart: "I am separate from you. My needs and my desires are more important than yours."

Everyone is born in that sinful isolation. But each is also breathed into being by a loving Creator who wills full flower for all creation. More powerfully than the human race's attraction to darkness is God's love for each and every person. God reaches out to gather all human children into loving arms.

Love is the bridge that closes the gap between persons. In love, another's need cannot be ignored. Your baby's need for food and comfort is your own need to soothe and nurture—even when it conflicts with your need for rest.

There is in the human heart a hunger for goodness, a need to see and touch kindness, thoughtfulness, generosity. That hunger is part of the hopes you hold for your child, part of the vision held by the believing community. It is intimately part of the dream God spins for us. God continues to speak love, calling us back to the vision of a united family. Divine love builds a bridge across the distances people create.

Goodness does not come easily. Generosity is costly and love a lot of hard work. Thoughtfulness is a minute-to-minute decision. Growth in goodness is a daily effort that begins with a fundamental choice, a profound decision against evil.

Baptism expresses that choice with a solemn promise to reject evil and live in the love and beauty God planned for creation. Baptism reverses the ancient refusal to respond with love to a loving Creator.

Original Sin

The story of the forbidden fruit in Genesis may be figurative, but its message is undeniable. Just as your child may apparently inherit your weaknesses and as surely as he or she will imitate your lapses from grace, all of us share in the sin of our first parents. "Original sin" casts its shadow over everyone.

No baby can make such a choice or consciously consider the alternatives. A toddler respects your treasures only because you demand it. A young child makes a thoughtful gesture for the smiling reward it brings. An older child's sense of justice depends on peer pressure; friends will exclude one who cheats from the game. And over-tired babies have been known to ignore their parents' need for sleep on the very night of their Baptism.

An infant is not capable of choosing goodness over evil consciously and independently. But you can, for the time being, speak for your child.

You make fundamental choices for your little one. You choose health, and your baby wails at the prick of a needle. You choose knowledge, and your child must struggle with math facts and phonics. You choose values, and a very self-centered being learns to share cherished belongings and may not express rage violently.

Your baby's right to make free choices remains strong. He may drop out of school or harm the body whose health you have nurtured with such care. Beyond doubt, the independent person for whom you renounce sin will be, at times, selfish and thoughtless and hurtful to others.

Life and health, knowledge and goodness are not really yours to give. All you can offer is a beginning. But a good beginning is a gift of love.

Baptism guarantees growth in faith and love no more than the first series of shots guarantees lifelong health. In making a commitment for your child, you commit your-self to nurturing growth. The dimensions of that commit-ment will unfold with unexpected delight and surprising disappointment. Like the substitute teacher who is just a chapter ahead of the students, you may find that you must continually probe your own religious understanding in order to nurture your child's beliefs.

It just could be a wondrous adventure for both of

you! Teaching and example, admonition and honest sharing are the tools that shape the fulfillment of your baby's baptismal promises. But first comes the simple joy of holding a little body in your arms and crooning foolish affection. Your love first enables this baby to become as loving and lovable as God intended.

For Reflection and Discussion

- *What effects of sin do you see most clearly in the world? In your own life?*

- *Why are you willing to bring a child into such a world?*

- *What is your greatest fear for your child? What evil do you most hope to keep from your baby?*

- *What religious values do you most hope to pass on to your child?*

Do you reject sin, so as to live in the freedom of God's children?

Do you reject the glamor of evil, and refuse to be mastered by sin?

Do you reject Satan, father of sin and prince of darkness? (*Rite of Baptism*, 94)

When Israel was a child I loved him,
and out of Egypt I called my son.
The more I called them,
the more they went from me;
they kept sacrificing to Baals,
and offering incense to idols.

Yet it was I who taught Ephraim to walk,
I took them up in my arms
but they did not know that I healed them.
I led them with cords of human kindness,
with bands of love.
I was to them like those
who lift infants to their cheeks.
I bent down to them and fed them.
(Hosea 11:1-4)

Born with a fallen human nature and tainted by original sin, children also have need of the new birth in Baptism to be freed from the power of darkness and brought into the realm of the freedom of the children of God.... Christian parents will recognize that this practice also accords with their role as nurturers of the life that God has entrusted to them. (*Catechism of the Catholic Church*, #1250-1251)

Alive in
Jesus Christ

When a child is lost, friends, neighbors and police join the search. But no parent wants to sit and wait for word without taking part in the search.

In the beginning, says the Bible, darkness lay over a formless wasteland until God's breath warmed it with life. But God's favorite creatures turned again and again to darkness. As the human refusal to warm with divine love spread its dark chill over the face of the earth, God came in person to find the children.

In Jesus Christ, the gap between God and human children closed at last. One person lived in perfect harmony with God's plan; one life was poured out in love for the rest of the family. Jesus brought God's plan to fulfillment. He broke the chains of mortality and gained new and lasting life, laying clear the pattern intended for all human life.

Baptism is dying and rising with Jesus Christ. It is not easy to speak of death when you still check your sleeping baby's breath. But it is never easy to speak of death without also speaking of resurrection.

The baptismal font is the sea from which new life emerges. Three times the baptized sink below the water; three times it flows over a baby's head. And human life, with its limits and its potential for evil, is laid down. With the crucified Jesus, your baby surrenders the gift of life into the hands of the Giver.

In Jesus, God walked the path of laughter and tears all people must travel. In Jesus, God established a new relationship with family, becoming not only parent but also brother.

Jesus' death opened a way through the doors of death into life beyond all limits for him and for all people. Faithful to the divine dream for the human family, Jesus drew so close to his brothers and sisters that he can carry them with him into new and lasting life.

Source of Grace

We speak of the sacraments as the source of sanctifying grace. The first definition the dictionary gives for *grace* is "favor," and a great favor it is! God freely fills us with divine life—everlasting life. This gift "sanctifies" us; it makes us holy.

Human beings are shaped by the people who love them. This child who lives in your love will grow in your likeness. Your attitudes, your expressions, your mannerisms will become part of who your baby is. Brothers and sisters do not always look alike, but those who know one well discover in the others a resemblance that goes deeper than facial similarity.

People who let themselves be loved by Jesus Christ grow in his likeness, too. So intimate is his relationship with his brothers and sisters that believers can speak of discovering him in each other. They even take his name as their own.

This name, too, becomes your child's at Baptism. She becomes a Christian, another Christ living in the world. With the other members of God's family, your child will learn to pray in Jesus' name, knowing that God surely hears the voices of children so closely identified with the beloved Son.

And so a new creation rises from the baptismal waters. Your child begins a new life with Jesus, one which cannot be cut short except by his own conscious choice. Once again, divine and human meet in a single life that lights the world anew.

Now the Son whose life was a perfect yes to God can speak a fresh affirmative. Now the man who walked Israel can wander your town, continuing to heal and forgive through your child. The face of Jesus wears a smile never seen before; his voice is new.

Life in Jesus Christ is God's greatest gift. To bring your baby for Baptism is to share that gift, to invite your child to join with you in unwrapping God's love.

For Reflection and Discussion

- *What persons have had the greatest influence in shaping who you are?*

- *Is Jesus a real person to you, or just an idea? Who has helped to make him real to you?*

- *How would you recognize Jesus in a crowd? From whom did you acquire that image?*

Receive the light of Christ. Parents and god-parents, this light is entrusted to you to be kept burning brightly. This child of yours has been enlightened by Christ. He (she) is to walk always as a child of the light. May he (she) keep the flame of faith alive in his (her) heart. When the Lord comes, may he (she) go out to meet him with all the saints in the heavenly kingdom. (*Rite of Baptism*, 100)

See what love the Father has given us, that we should be called children of God; and that is what we are. The reason the world does not know us is that it did not know him. Beloved, we are God's children now; what we will be has not yet been revealed. What we do know is this: when he is revealed, we will be like him, for we will see him as he is. (1 John 3:1-2)

Having received in Baptism the Word, "the true light that enlightens every man," the person baptized has been "enlightened," he becomes a "son of light," indeed, he becomes "light" himself. (*Catechism of the Catholic Church*, #1216)

The Language of Celebration

When words are inadequate, people speak in gestures and signs: a hug, a touch, a gift. The language of ritual enables people to share events words cannot express.

God's action is no more limited to sacramental actions than the whole of married love is lived out in the marriage bed. But the sacraments, like lovemaking, are moments of intensified encounter.

In any such exchange, the more expressive the gestures and symbols, the more eloquent the communication. The more meaning you intend a gift to convey, the more carefully you choose or make it.

Baptism speaks with water and light, oil and white garment, song, and sometimes even welcoming applause. The rite can speak as expressively as a tender embrace or as perfunctorily as a routine good-bye peck. Routine and tender moments both nourish love, but not the same way. One speaks of minimums, the other of possibilities.

Baptismal Symbols

Water is essential to life on earth. The water used in Baptism is blessed with a prayer that it will cleanse your child and bring him to new life. It can simply be poured over the child's head or your little one can be lowered into it.

The baby is anointed with **chrism**, a scented oil. It was blessed by the bishop, head of the larger church in your area, on Holy Thursday. Kings, priests and prophets were consecrated with oil in biblical times. Baptized, your child has a share in kingly, priestly and prophetic ministry.

The **white garment** symbolizes baptismal innocence. The child is urged to bring it unspotted to God's throne at the end of life.

The **baptismal candle** burns with the light of Christ. It is yours to keep; burn it on special days (birthdays, other sacramental occasions).

The options offered in the Rite of Baptism let you express the meanings you have discovered in the sacrament in a very personal way.

Parishes, like families, are not all alike. Their traditions vary. Some celebrate Baptism during Sunday Mass; others in a special afternoon Mass. Still others baptize without celebrating Eucharist.

Pouring water over an infant's head suffices, but babies can also be baptized by immersion, visibly going down into death with Jesus Christ.

Some parishes invite parents to choose the Scripture readings for their baby's Baptism from a selection of passages which contain God's promise of life.

The baptismal robe and candle can be made by parents, godparents or friends with skillful hands. If you have a christening dress handed down through the generations, clothing the child in it at the appropriate place in the rite speaks eloquently of passing on an inheritance.

What do you ask of God's Church for your baby? The question itself may be just the first of many you struggle to answer as you guide your child's growth in faith.

You are not alone. The Church prays with you for continued growth to uncontrollable glory:

By God's gift, through water and the Holy Spirit, we are reborn to everlasting life. In his goodness, may he continue to pour out his blessings upon these sons and daughters of his. May he make them always, wherever they may be, faithful members of his holy people. May he send his peace upon all who are gathered here, in Christ Jesus our Lord. (*Rite of Baptism*, 183)

For Reflection and Discussion

- *What white garment will your child wear? Will you make or purchase the baptismal candle yourself?*

- *Will the Baptism be celebrated at Sunday Mass or at some other time? Will the baby be immersed?*

- *What Scripture passages would you like to hear at your child's Baptism?*

Baptism is the sacrament of faith. But faith needs the community of believers. It is only within the faith of the Church that each of the faithful can believe. (*Catechism of the Catholic Church,* #1253)